Drawing

Sue Stocks

With photographs by Chris Fairclough

Thomson Learning • New York

FIRST ARTS & CRAFTS

Books in this series

Collage
Drawing
Masks
Models
Painting
Printing
Puppets
Toys and Games

For Tom and Kati

First published in the
United States in 1994 by
Thomson Learning
115 Fifth Avenue
New York, NY 10003

First published by Wayland (Publishers) Ltd.

Library of Congress Cataloging-in-Publication Data
Stocks, Sue.
  Drawing/Sue Stocks; with photographs by Chris Fairclough.
      p.   cm.—(First arts & crafts)
  Includes bibliographical references and index.
  ISBN 1-56847-211-0
  1. Drawing—Juvenile literature. [1. Drawing—Technique.]
I. Fairclough, Chris, ill. II. Title. III. Series: Stocks, Sue.
First arts & crafts.
NC655.S76   1994
741.2—dc20   94-374

Printed in Italy

Contents

Drawing materials

There are lots of different ways of drawing and many things with which you can draw. Thousands of years ago, cave people dipped their fingers or sticks into mud and drew pictures on the walls of their caves. In some countries people use their fingers to draw bright patterns on their faces and bodies. Children often use sticks to draw pictures in wet sand. In this book, we are going to try drawing with different materials.

You will need:

A variety of drawing materials, including different lead pencils, such as No. 1, 2, and 3 (the more the better), colored pencils, water-soluble pencils, charcoal sticks, wax crayons, pastels, colored felt-tipped pens, a fine-line black felt-tipped pen

Paper

Cave paintings by the San peoples, Matopos National Park, Zimbabwe, Africa.

- Get a large sheet of paper and a pencil.
- Start drawing a line across the paper. Turn left. Don't take your pencil off the paper. Keep going. Now turn right.
- Take your pencil for a walk across the paper in different directions. Cross some of the lines you have already made. Watch different shapes appear.
- Keep drawing until your paper is covered with lines.

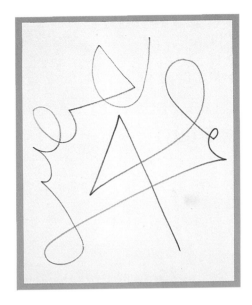

- Fill in the shapes you have made with different colors and black and white. Use all the pens, pencils, crayons, and the other drawing materials you have collected. Make dots in some shapes. Crisscross colors in other shapes.

When you have filled in all the shapes, look at the pattern they make.

Charcoal pencil patterns

In this picture of a horse and its rider, the artist has used lots of flowing lines.

Drawing for the Sforza Monument by Leonardo da Vinci (1452-1519). Crayon.

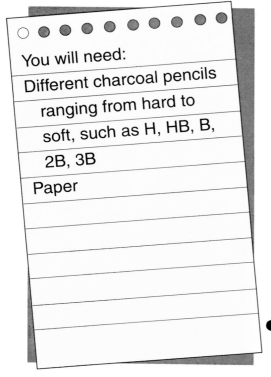

You will need:

Different charcoal pencils ranging from hard to soft, such as H, HB, B, 2B, 3B

Paper

Try drawing with your different pencils.

● Make a few lines with each pencil on a big sheet of paper. Draw large circles or other shapes. Use your whole arm as you draw.

Some of your lines will be pale. Some will be dark. Hard pencils make pale lines; soft pencils make dark ones. How can you tell the difference between your pencils? Look at the letters and numbers on your pencils. Hard pencils have the letter "H" on them. Soft pencils have the letter "B."

- Get two big sheets of paper. Tear several pieces out of one of them so that it is full of different-shaped holes. Lay this sheet on top of the other.
- With a pencil, fill in one of the shapes. Do it very lightly.
- Fill in another shape with the same pencil. This time, press harder. Are the lines darker?
- With another pencil, fill another shape with straight lines. Draw them close together and all going the same way. This is called hatching.
- Change pencils again. Fill another shape with lines. Then draw over those lines with a second set of lines going in a different direction. This is called cross-hatching.
- Use the side of the lead instead of the tip of another pencil to fill in another shape.

Use all your pencils in different ways to fill in all the shapes. Make wavy lines and dots. When you have finished, lift off the top sheet and see your pattern.

Leaf rubbings

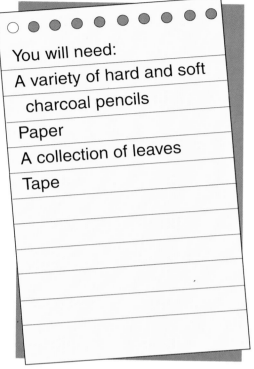

You will need:
A variety of hard and soft
 charcoal pencils
Paper
A collection of leaves
Tape

Look at the patterns and shapes of the leaves in your collection. Put the leaves in a row and look at them closely. Now put the leaves in order from light to dark, so that the lightest leaf comes first and the darkest leaf comes last.

- Choose three leaves and three charcoal pencils (an H, a B, and a 2B).
- Cover the leaves with a sheet of paper.
- With one of your pencils, gently rub the paper over one of the leaves. Use the side of the lead, not the top. Watch the outline of the leaf appear.
- Rub over the top of another leaf with a different pencil.
- Do the same with all the leaves and pencils.

The leaves on your paper will be light and dark.

Look at this picture of leaves floating on a pond. What else can you see in the water?

Now you are going to draw your leaves. Put them close together. Look carefully at the shapes. What else can you see? Look at the lines and patterns on the leaves.

- Choose a leaf to draw.
- Use a soft pencil.
- Draw the outline of the leaf first.
- Now draw the lines on the leaf. Fill in the leaf to show the light and dark areas. Do it very gently.

Three Worlds – 1955 by M. C. Escher (1898-1972). Print.

Try drawing all your leaves. When you have finished, cut the drawings out and tape them to colored paper.

Pastel bubbles

Try drawing with your colored pastels on different colored papers.

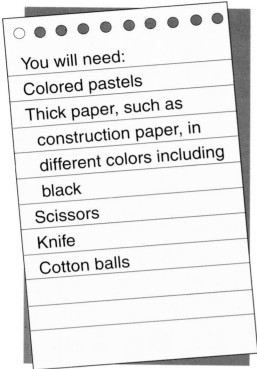

- Choose a sheet of colored paper. Try all your colored pastels on the paper.
- Pick another color of paper and use your pastels again. Make big shapes and lines.
- Choose a light colored pastel to fill in one of the big shapes.
- With a darker color, draw over half of the first color. Don't press too hard. See how the colors mix.
- Fill in some more shapes with other pastel colors.

Look at this pastel picture. See how the artist has put different colors on top of one another. You can do the same in your pictures.

- Cut out a small circle from a sheet of paper. Now you have a stencil. Lay it over a piece of paper.
- Ask an adult to help you scrape some chalk from the side of a pastel with a knife or a blade of the scissors.
- Dip the cotton ball into the chalk powder and rub it over the stencil.
- Add more powder to one half of the circle for a shadow effect.

Le Bain by Edgar Degas (1834-1917). Pastel.

Lift off the stencil and look at the shape underneath. With the stencil, make lots of different-colored bubbles on the same piece of paper.

Make a sheet of different-shaped stencils.

11

Masks and headdresses

Look at these photographs. They are of masks and headdresses from different countries. Some are from festivals.

Tribal masks are sometimes made for special dances. Others are made to frighten enemies away. You can draw your own mask.

You will need:

Colored pastels

Large sheets of black construction paper

Pictures of festivals, headdresses, and tribal masks

- Choose a mask or a headdress from these photographs or from pictures you've found.
- Draw the mask or headdress with your pastels. Start at the top of the paper and work down.
- Keep looking at the picture you have chosen to draw. Use bright colors.

When you have finished your drawing, hang it on the wall.

You can create your own mask. Will it be smiling or fierce? Look in a mirror and smile. See the shape of your mouth, eyes, and eyebrows. Now frown and see how those shapes change.

- Use your pastels to draw the outline of your mask. Make it big.
- Draw in the nose, eyes, and mouth.
- Decorate your mask with lots of colors. Blend them by drawing one color over another and then rubbing with your finger.

Draw a mask with a different mood. Hang it next to the first one you made.

13

Birthday party

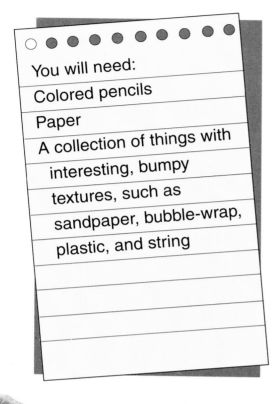

You will need:

Colored pencils

Paper

A collection of things with interesting, bumpy textures, such as sandpaper, bubble-wrap, plastic, and string

Use your colored pencils on a sheet of paper to make patches of different colors next to one another. Which color do you like best?

Colored pencils are different from pastels. Try drawing and shading with your colored pencils. Try blending the colors by putting one on top of another, just as you did with the pastels. Do they look the same when you blend them?

Now make some rubbings with the things you collected.

- Put some sandpaper under a piece of drawing paper.
- Rub a colored pencil gently over the top of the paper over the sandpaper. Use the side of the lead and try to rub smoothly – don't scribble! Watch how the marks appear.

- Make more rubbings of the sandpaper with other colors.
- Now put a piece of string under the paper and make another rubbing.
- Do the same with all the things you collected.

Artists sometimes make pictures like this. It is called frottage.

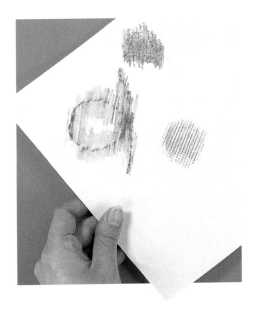

Now draw a picture. Draw a birthday party. It could be one of your birthday parties or one you have been to. You could draw the table with the cake and all the other food on it. You could draw the presents wrapped up in colorful papers. What else could you draw?

- Draw your picture on a big sheet of paper. Keep it simple.
- Choose the colors you are going to use. Think about the things you could put under your paper to make interesting marks in your picture. You could use string for hair, or sandpaper for the wrapping paper.

15

Look at this picture. It is by a famous English artist and sculptor named Henry Moore. Look at the shapes of the people.

Pink and Green Sleepers 1941 by Henry Moore (1898-1986). Pen and ink, chalk, crayon, and wash.

You can draw a picture of your family or friends. Try drawing with charcoal first.

- Draw big circles and ovals with your charcoal sticks and pencils on a large sheet of paper. Use your whole arm when you draw. Do you like using the sticks or the pencils better?
- Draw people, using a circle for the head and an oval for the body. Try not to rest your arm on your drawing or you will smudge the charcoal.

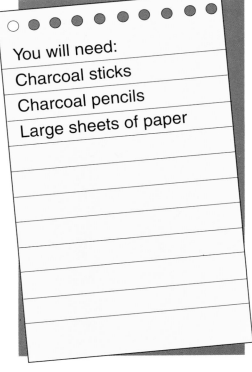

You will need:

Charcoal sticks

Charcoal pencils

Large sheets of paper

When you have practiced drawing with charcoal, draw some of your friends or family. Choose two or three of them. Ask them to stand together in front of you. Are they all the same size? Look at the shapes of their bodies. Start to draw. Keep looking at the people as you draw. Make your drawing very big.

Tropical birds

This is another drawing by Henry Moore, the artist and sculptor who drew the people on page 16. He used wax crayons to make parts of this picture.

Another book in this series, called *Painting*, shows you how to make pictures with a wax resist.

Mother and Child Scene 1978 by Henry Moore. Pencil, charcoal, chalk, wax crayon, and wash.

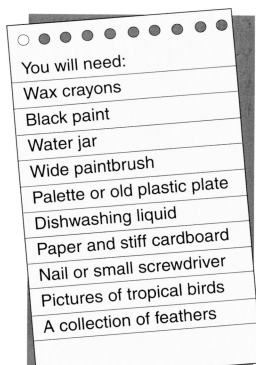

You will need:

Wax crayons

Black paint

Water jar

Wide paintbrush

Palette or old plastic plate

Dishwashing liquid

Paper and stiff cardboard

Nail or small screwdriver

Pictures of tropical birds

A collection of feathers

- Draw a picture with wax crayons.
- Brush some thin black paint lightly over the top. See how the wax resists the paint.

Now use the wax crayons in a different way.

- Cut out a small piece of cardboard.
- Color the entire piece with wax crayons. Use lots of colors and build up a very thick layer of wax.
- Mix some thick black paint. Stir in a squeeze of dishwashing liquid.
- Brush the black paint thickly over the cardboard.
- When the paint is dry, use a nail or screwdriver to scratch patterns through the black. Watch the colors appear underneath. This way of drawing is called sgraffito.

Look at these photographs of colorful birds.

Use sgraffito to make your own bright picture of a bird on a big sheet of cardboard. Look at pictures of birds and at the lines and patterns on the feathers you have collected. Will the feathers on your bird be like these? Make lots of different marks through the black paint to give your bird interesting texture.

Fruits and vegetables

Some paintings are made out of dots. This technique is called pointillism. You can use felt-tipped pens to make pictures out of dots. You can use them to draw in different ways.

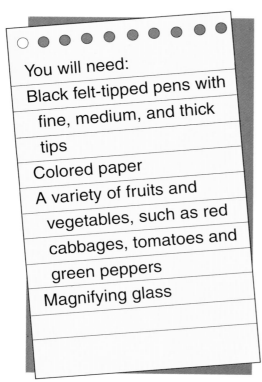

You will need:

Black felt-tipped pens with fine, medium, and thick tips

Colored paper

A variety of fruits and vegetables, such as red cabbages, tomatoes and green peppers

Magnifying glass

- Make some dots with the different pens on a sheet of paper. Keep some of the dots close together. Spread others out.
- Draw some small shapes and fill them with dots.
- Now draw some lines close together.
- Draw more lines and cross over them with other lines. You have done this before with pencil. It is called cross-hatching. Does it look different when it is done with felt-tipped pens?

Look at this piece of red cabbage.
Can you see the lovely patterns made by the wavy lines?

- Choose a thick pen and a large sheet of colored paper.
- Look at the light and dark parts of the cabbage. Look at them again through a magnifying glass.
- Using only dots, try to draw the patterns you see.

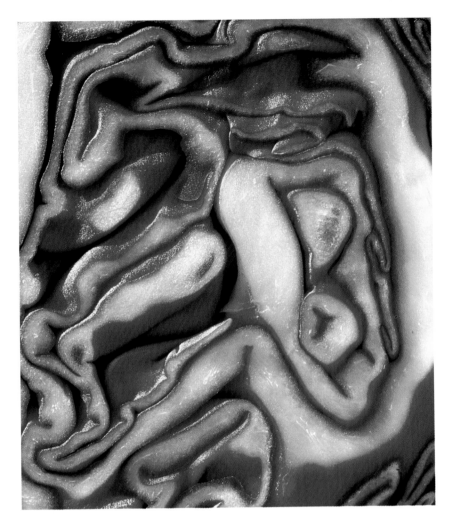

Now draw the cabbage again. Try using cross-hatching this time, or just make thick and thin lines with your pens. Keep looking at the pattern of the cabbage.

Ask an adult to help you cut some other vegetables and fruits in half. Draw the patterns you see.

Make some drawings like this with different-colored pens.

Watercolor pencils

You can use watercolor pencils in different ways.

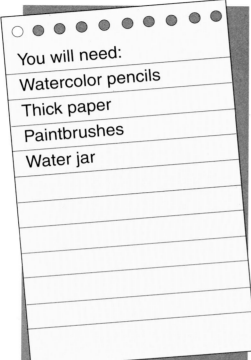

You will need:

Watercolor pencils

Thick paper

Paintbrushes

Water jar

- On white paper, practice drawing with the watercolor pencils.
- Now draw each letter in your name with different colors. Dip a paintbrush in water and brush it over the letters. Watch the colors spread.
- Draw the letters again, but this time dip the tips of your pencils in the water first.
- Wet some paper with a brush dipped in water. Draw the letters on the damp paper.

You have tried four ways of drawing with watercolor pencils. How are they different from regular colored pencils? Remember that you can mix and match them too. Use these pencils to draw a view through a window. You can be looking in or out of the window.

Look at this picture. Where do you think it might be? Your window picture could be of a vacation or a beach view.

Think about the different shapes of windows you see. Will your picture be looking out a round or square window? What might you see? Draw your window picture in one of the four ways you learned to use your watercolor pencils.

Still Life with Fish and Fruit by Raoul Dufy (1877-1953). Oil on linen cloth.

Make a different window picture and use another way of drawing with watercolor pencils. Hang your two windows together on the wall.

Impressing

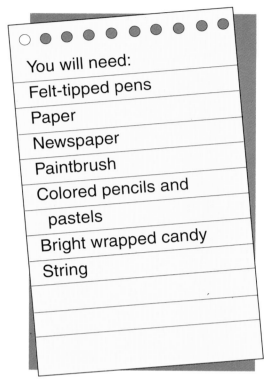

You will need:

Felt-tipped pens

Paper

Newspaper

Paintbrush

Colored pencils and
 pastels

Bright wrapped candy

String

Practice drawing with your felt-tipped pens. Use some of the different techniques you have learned in this book.

- Lay a sheet of drawing paper over some folded newspaper.
- Use a paintbrush handle to draw an invisible picture on the drawing paper. Press hard.
- Hatch lightly over your "drawing" with a felt-tipped pen. Watch the picture appear.

Try this again, using a crayon or pastel instead of a felt-tipped pen. This way of drawing is called impressing.

- Color some paper with a felt-tipped pen.
- Lay the paper over the folded newspaper and draw another picture with the paintbrush handle.
- Color lightly over the top with a darker crayon or pastel. Does this look different from the first picture you did?

- Choose some brightly wrapped candies. Put one in front of you.
- Draw the candy using the impressing technique. Make it big. Draw any patterns or creases in the candy wrapper.
- Draw more candies like this.
- Now draw some candies using just the felt-tipped pens. Use lots of colors.

When you have finished, cut out your candies and string them together.

Portraits

This drawing is a portrait. For a very long time, people have had their portraits painted by famous artists. Sometimes, artists paint pictures of themselves. These are called self-portraits.

Portraits and self-portraits that were painted many years ago tell us about the way the people lived and what their jobs were. Their clothes and pets, as well as objects and things happening in the pictures, tell us something. Many years ago, there were no cameras to take photographs of people.

The Mother by Charles White (1918-1979). Ink.

You can draw a portrait. Think what will be in the picture. Whom will you draw? Will the person look happy or serious? Look at the person closely. What color hair does he or she have? What are the clothes like? What else will you put in the picture with the person – a favorite toy or a family pet? Put in the things that remind you of that person.

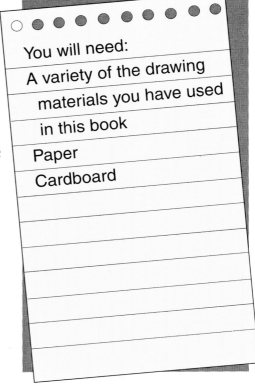

You will need:
A variety of the drawing materials you have used in this book
Paper
Cardboard

- Use a large sheet of paper and a pencil, pastel, or whatever drawing material you like best. You could use a few different materials in the same picture.

- Sit in front of the person you are going to draw.
- Draw the person from top to bottom, starting with the head.
- Keep looking at the person as you draw.
- Add the background.

Make a cardboard frame for your portrait and paint or draw on that, too.

Black and white

You will need:

Scratchboard

A scratchboard tool or something with a sharp point, such as a darning needle or nail

A black felt-tipped pen

White paper

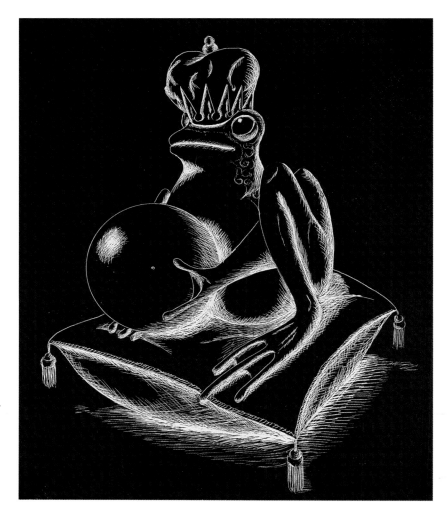

This picture was drawn on scratchboard.

With a sharp tool, practice making different lines and marks on a piece of scratchboard. Watch the white lines appear as you scrape the black away. Think of all the lines and marks you have tried in this book – dots, lines, cross-hatched lines, zigzags. Try them all. Think of some more. Try out your own ideas.

Your picture is going to be black and white. Think of a favorite story or poem and draw a picture of something that happens in it. Try to make it interesting. Make lots of marks in the scratchboard to show different textures.

When you have finished, draw another picture of the same scene. This time, draw it on white paper with a black felt-tipped pen. Try to make it the same as the first picture. Now look at the two together. You have black on white and white on black. Do they look different?

Hang them together on a wall.

29

Helpful hints

There are all kinds of fancy pencils and papers available at art supply stores. But an artist can make a good drawing with a No. 2 pencil and scrap paper. Practice and a good imagination are two of the most important tools a person needs to make drawings. Use your imagination when you think about what to draw and how you'll draw it. Let drawings in museums, books, and magazines give you ideas. Draw things you see every day, such as your home, the view from your bedroom window, or a friend's face. And practice, practice, practice!

Here are some helpful hints:

- Brown parcel paper, scrap paper, and even newspaper make good surfaces on which to practice drawing.

- Decorate a coffee can or large jar and use it to store your pencils.

- Draw with a white crayon on black paper for a different effect.

- Draw the same thing twice – once with a hard pencil and once with a soft pencil. Compare the results.

- When practicing, draw on both sides of your paper to make it last. Cut big sheets of paper in half.

- Set up a gallery on your bedroom wall. You can put your drawings in inexpensive plastic frames, tack them to a bulletin board, or use plastic adhesive to hang them on a wall.

- Ask a friend to draw with you.

Glossary

Charcoal A black substance made from burned wood. It can be made into sticks or pencils for drawing.

Creases Lines left in paper that has been folded or crumpled.

Festivals Special days or times during which people celebrate something.

Frame The border around a picture or window.

Headdresses Decorated headgear sometimes worn during festivals.

Pastels Crayons made from colored powders that are pressed and stuck together. The crayons look like colored chalk.

Pattern Shapes and colors that are repeated.

Portrait A picture of a person or animal.

Sculptor An artist who makes works of art (called sculptures) in solid materials such as wood, metal, or stone. You can usually see sculptures from every side.

Self-portrait A portrait of oneself.

Techniques Ways of doing something. In this book, they are different ways of drawing.

Texture The feel or look of a surface.

Tribal masks Tribes are groups of people who share the same way of life and beliefs. In some places, such as Africa and South America, they may make and wear masks for special days or activities.

Watercolor pencils Pencils that become watery when they are wet so that you can paint as well as draw with them.

Wax resist Using wax to keep areas free of paint.

Further information

Further reading

DuBosque, Doug. *Learn to Draw 3-D.* Molalla, OR: Peel Productions, 1992.

Hodge, Anthony. *Drawing.* Hands On Arts and Crafts. New York: Gloucester Press, 1991.

LaPlaca, Micheal. *How to Draw Cars and Trucks.* Mahwah, NJ: Troll Associates, 1982.

McKay, Bob. *How to Draw Funny People.* Mahwah, NJ: Troll Associates, 1981.

Index

Acknowledgments

The publishers wish to thank the following for the use of photographs:
Visual Arts Library for M.C. Escher's *Three Worlds – 1955,* © 1955 M.C. Escher Foundation ® – Baarn – Holland, all rights reserved; Leonardo da Vinci's *Drawing for the Sforza Monument,* The Royal Collection; Edgar Degas' *Le Bain,* Private Collection; Charles White's *The Mother,* Hirshhorn Museum, Smithsonian; and Raoul Dufy's *Still Life with Fish and Fruit* © DACS 1994.
Reproduced by kind permission of the Henry Moore Foundation: *Second Shelter Sketchbook 1941, Sleeping Child Covered with Blanket* (front cover) © Henry Moore Foundation (year of first publication); *Pink and Green Sleepers 1941* © Henry Moore Foundation (year of first publication); *Mother and Child Scene 1978* © Henry Moore Foundation (year of first publication).
Additional photographs reproduced by kind permission of Chris Fairclough Colour Library.

The publishers also wish to thank our models Anna and Jeremy, and our young artists Sue, Rebecca, and Inigo.